The Basketball Scoring Guide

by   Sidney Goldstein

author of **The Basketball Coach's Bible**

and **The Basketball Player's Bible**

GOLDEN AURA PUBLISHING

The Nitty-Gritty Basketball Series

The Basketball Scoring Guide
by Sidney Goldstein

Published by:

GOLDEN AURA PUBLISHING

Post Office Box 41012

Philadelphia, PA 19127 U.S.A.

Library of Congress Card Number   98- 75682

Goldstein, Sidney

The Basketball Scoring Guide

Sidney Goldstein.--Second Edition, 1999

Basketball-Coaching

ISBN 1-884357-31-8

Softcover

Contents

Introduction

Over many years of coaching, planning, and studying, I found ways to teach each and every skill even to the most unskilled player. This scheme of learning did not come from any book. I tried things in practice. I modified them till they worked. Even players who could not simultaneously chew bubble gum and walk learned the skills. This booklet, part of **The Nitty-Gritty Basketball Series**, is one result of this effort. I believe you can benefit from my work.

Who Can Use This Information

This booklet is the perfect tool for anybody who wants to coach, teach, and/or learn basketball:

- A parent who wants to teach his or her child
- A player who wants to understand and play the game better
- A little league or recreation league coach
- A high school or junior high school coach
- A college coach, a professional coach
- A women's or a men's coach

This booklet contains material from **The Basketball Player's Bible**. Chapter 1 gives the keys to learning the skills presented. I present the skills in lesson form. Chapter 2 gives the features of each lesson. The largest chapter, Chapter 3, presents the lessons in order. Check the **Lessons Needed Before** feature as you progress.

Most of the lessons in this guide are called moves, or scoring moves. Most involve pivoting and faking with a short shot. Pressure shooting lessons are also included. These lessons put you in game-type situations in practice. You should practice shooting and pivoting technique before you work on moves. **The Basketball Player's Bible** contains the lessons presented here and many other related ones.

Golden Aura's Nitty-Gritty Basketball Series
by Sidney Goldstein

See the description in the back of this book.

The Basketball Coach's Bible

The Basketball Player's Bible

The Basketball Shooting Guide

The Basketball Scoring Guide

The Basketball Dribbling Guide

The Basketball Defense Guide

The Basketball Pass Cut Catch Guide

Basketball Fundamentals

Planning Basketball Practice

Videos for the Guides soon available

HOW TO CONTACT THE AUTHOR

The author seeks your comments about this book. Sidney Goldstein is available for consultation and clinics with coaches and players. Contact him at:

Golden Aura Publishing
PO Box 41012
Philadelphia, PA 19127
215 438-4459

Chapter One

1

Principles of Learning

How To Use The Shooting Guide

Start from the beginning and progress through the lessons one by one. Typically, I arrange them in order of increasing difficulty. You may want to skip some topics. However, use the **Lessons Needed Before** feature to insure that you do not omit needed techniques.

The most important as well as the most frequently skipped lessons involve techniques. If you spend the needed time on these lessons, you will improve exponentially on a daily basis. Skip them and improvement may be delayed for months and even years.

One big misconception about learning the basics is that to improve you must practice things millions of times. I've tried it and so has everybody else. It does not work well. Volume of practice does not necessarily bring about improvement; practicing properly insures improvement. The following **principles** tell you what and how to practice. A list of **Counterproductive Beliefs** follows. These often widely held ideas prevent learning because they do not work.

Note that the moves in this guide are more advanced skills than shooting. Moves involve pivoting, shooting, and faking as well as ball handling skills. I suggest that you practice moves only after these skills are up to par.

The principles of moves are the same as the principles of shooting.

The Principles Of Shooting

1. Shooting improvement starts with technique.

2. Technique must be practiced close to the basket.

3. To improve your shooting range start close to the basket and gradually back off.

4. To improve shooting you must shoot in a game-like situation. See lessons 12-15.

5. Every shooting move, as will as every other move to dribble or to pass, starts with a pivot. So, you must be an expert at pivoting. See Lesson 16.

Counterproductive Beliefs

1. Repetition yields improvement. This is only true to a limited degree. Improvement only follows doing things correctly. Practicing incorrectly yields problems. If you practice correctly, follow the lessons, improvement will come with much less repetition than you initially thought.

2. Only 7th graders need to practice technique. Not true. Even Hall of Famers do. Every time you play ball you need to warm up with a few minutes of shooting technique.

3. Only 7th graders need to practice close to the basket. No, everybody does for several reasons. One is that this is the best way to use and apply technique. And again I say, without technique improvement, there is no improvement. The other reason is that a great percentage of shots are taken from this area in a game. So, it is most beneficial to practice game level shooting especially in this area.

4. You can work on technique as you work on shooting. Nope. Technique and shooting need to be practiced separately. One, technique improves your shot by changing and focusing on the mechanics (movement) of the shot. You give little thought to the actual shot when working on technique. Conversely or inversely or reciprocally, thinking about technique when in the motion of shooting can only psyche you out. These two things should be practiced, and even more importantly, thought about separately.

5. If you are a good shooter in practice, then you should be a good game shooter. No. Shooting rested, under little psychological pressure or physical defensive pressure in practice is not the same as shooting under more adverse game situations. Good shooters are good game shooters.

6. You need talent to shoot well. Only naturally talented players can shoot well and learn tricky moves. Not so. Anybody can be a good shooter or dribbler, passer, etc., if they practice properly.

7. Great shooters are great players. Not so. Note that many Hall of Famers are not great shooters. Shooting is only one part of the game. If you want to be a great basketball player, you need to be as tall, strong, quick, and fast as possible. Work on being an athlete as well as practicing the skills. All Hall of Famers are great athletes.

Chapter Two

2

Lesson Features

Table Information

At a glance this table gives an overview to aid in planning. It supplies the name and number of each lesson as well as these additional features: lessons needed before, the number of players needed, the effort level, the estimated practice times, whether you need a ball and/or a court. Practice the *no ball* or *no court* lessons for homework while watching TV or sitting down. The Player's Corner section of each lesson supplies some of the same information.

Number

The lessons are numbered in order from easiest to hardest, from most fundamental to most complicated. Typically, do them in order. Sometimes you can skip. If you do, check the **Lessons Needed Before** feature so that you do not skip essential lessons.

Name

A name related to each lesson serves as a descriptive mnemonic device (I almost forgot that). When skills are executed simultaneously, their names are directly coupled like Pivot Around Shoot or Jump Hook. Lessons with skills separately performed are named, for example, Pivot with Defense, where one player pivots on offense while the other is on defense.

Brief

In one sentence (usually) the **brief** immediately familiarizes you with the lesson by stating the action and movement involved.

Why Do This

When do you use this in a game? What is the significance of the lesson? What fundamentals do you practice? How does this lesson relate to others? The **Why Do This** section answers these questions.

Directions

These are step-by-step directions for you.

Key Points

This feature emphasizes important points in the directions so that you will not make common mistakes.

When You Are More Expert

These more expert lessons usually add another step, combine another skill, or change one variable in the previous lesson. Some lessons have as many as four expert additions.

Player's Corner and Section Tables

At a glance you can see that the **Player's Corner** lists 8 useful pieces of information about each lesson. The **Table of Lessons** in **Appendix C** and each **Section Table** contain this same information. **Xs** in the tables mean <u>yes</u>. Dashes (-) mean <u>no</u>.

• Lessons Needed Before

Do these lessons before this current one. If you don't, then you will have a problem. Often you can skip lessons without it being disastrous. Not so with the lessons listed as Lessons Needed Before.

• Additional Needs

This feature gives 4 useful pieces of information.

Ball and Court

For most lessons you need a **ball** and a **court**. However, for some either one or the other or both are not needed. These lessons can be practiced at home while watching TV or in your backyard. **Xs** in the tables mean <u>yes</u>.

Players

Most lessons are for individuals. So, the Player's Corner lists additional players needed, whereas the Tables give the total number (which is always one more than additional players).

Assist

For some lessons you need an inactive **assistant** to either act as a dummy player or more importantly to closely watch what you are doing. **Xs** in the tables mean <u>yes</u>.

• Effort or Effort Level

The effort level of a lesson involves the physical effort involved. Level 1 lessons involve technique. Do them slowly;

they often do not resemble the skill performed in a game because 2 to 5 technique lessons often comprise a skill. In situations calling for defense, the defense expends little effort.

Level 2 lessons are at the practice level. Any skill practiced at a moderate pace like shooting or pivoting is at level 2. This level is a catchall for lessons between levels 1 and 3. Defense against offense makes a moderate effort.

Level 3 lessons are at the game level. Players sprint and perform at maximum effort. Pressure is on players. Offense and defense go full speed against each other. Games are easy compared to these lessons.

• Daily Practice Time

This is a time range needed to practice this lesson. Note that many lessons have additional parts. These will take more time.

• More Expert Lessons

Each of these additions adds one or two parameters to the main lesson. Few are optional. Most need to be done after you are more expert.

FEATURES OF THE DIAGRAMS

Lines and Arrows

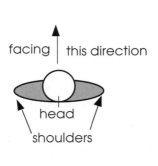

Solid lines indicate movement of players whereas dashed lines usually indicate movement of the ball. One exception is dashed lines used to show pivoting direction. The types of arrows used are solid for movement and hollow for passes. A different type of arrow head is used for fakes. See the diagrams.

Body Position of Player

The body of a player is shown from an overhead view two ways. The line or the ellipse represents the shoulders. The

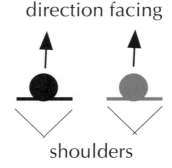

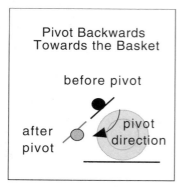

Pivot Backwards
Towards the Basket

before pivot

after pivot

pivot direction

circle shows the head. The player is always facing away from the shoulders toward the head.

Shades for Different Positions

When a player is shown in two positions in the same diagram, the first position is black and the second is lighter in color. Often offense or defense are shown in light and dark shades. In some diagrams shades are used to designate the position of a player when the ball of the same shade is in the diagramed position.

Numbers in Multistep Movements

Many drills involve multiple steps. Each step, as well, may have several timed movements that need to be executed in order. So, in the diagrams for each step, the numbers indicate the order of the movements. One (1) means first, two (2) second and so on. If two players move at the same time the numbers will be the same, so there may be several ones or twos in the diagram.

In the diagram below, there are three ones in the diagram. This indicates that these players move at the same time. There are two twos; one indicates a cut, while the other indicates a pass.

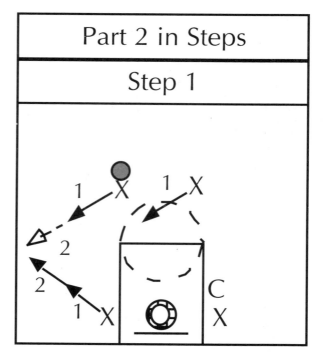

Chapter Three
3

Moves
Lessons 1-14

L E S S O N	NAME	A S S I S T	P L A Y E R S	C O U R T	B A L L	E F F O R T	L E S S O N	Lessons Before	REF TO Coach's Manual	DAILY TIME	E X T R A
1-16	**MOVES**										
1	Moves-Lessons 14-23	-	x	x	x	-	1	16	6.0	-	0
2	Pivot Around Shoot	-	1	x	x	1-2	2	1	6.1	5-20	0
3	Pivot Backward Shoot	-	1	x	x	1-2	3	2	6.2	5-20	0
4	Step Fake Shoot	-	1	x	x	1-2	4	2	6.3	5-20	0
5	Fake Pivot Shoot	-	1	x	x	1-2	5	4	6.31	5-20	1
6	Pivot Fake Shoot	-	1	x	x	1-2	6	4	6.4	5-20	1
7	Hook Shot 1-2	x	1	x	x	1-2	7	4	6.5	5-20	0
8	Jump Hook & Fake	-	1	x	x	1-2	8	7	6.51	5-20	2
9	Step Hook & Fake	-	1	x	x	1-2	9	8	6.53	5-20	2
10	Underneath Hooks	-	1	x	x	1-2	10	9	6.55	5-20	2
11	Jump Shot	-	1	x	x	1-2	11	4	6.6	5-20	4
12	Pressure Shot	x	1	x	x	2-3	12	11	7.0	5-15	2
13	Run Stop Shoot	x	1	x	x	2-3	13	12	7.1	2-5	2
14	Catch Up	x	2	x	x	3	14	12	7.2	5	0
15	Defense in Face Shoot	-	2	x	x	2-3	15	none	7.3	2-5	2
16	Pivoting with Ball	x	1	-	x	2	16	none	2.1	2-20	0

1 Moves

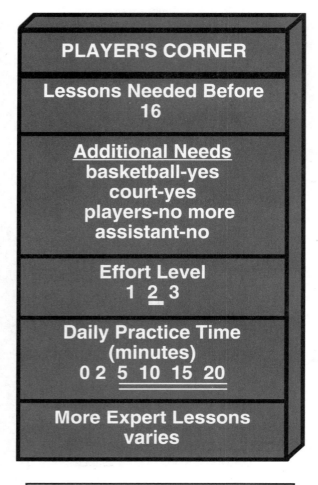

PLAYER'S CORNER

Lessons Needed Before
16

Additional Needs
basketball-yes
court-yes
players-no more
assistant-no

Effort Level
1 <u>2</u> 3

**Daily Practice Time
(minutes)**
0 2 <u>5</u> <u>10</u> <u>15</u> <u>20</u>

More Expert Lessons
varies

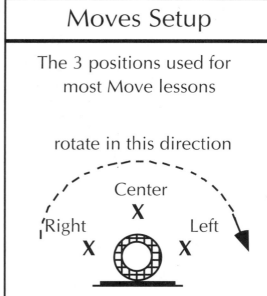

Moves Setup

The 3 positions used for
most Move lessons

rotate in this direction

Center
X
Right   Left
X   X

Brief:

All moves combine faking and pivoting with shooting. The information in this lesson applies to each lesson in this section.

Why Do This

Even though players execute moves from anywhere on the court, practice them one foot from the basket. The various fakes introduced can be used in many other situations.

These things vary in each move:

1. Direction of the pivot—forward (same direction as walking) or backward (like walking backward).

2. The starting direction—facing the basket, with the back to the basket, or underneath the basket.

3. Three types of fakes are used:

  •The ball body fake or ball fake involves faking toward the pivot foot with the ball and the body.

  •If a step is taken away from the pivot foot with this fake, it is called a ball body step fake or just a step fake.

  •When a pivot is used as a fake, call it a pivot fake instead of a ball body step pivot fake.

4. The shots include regular one foot shots, hook shots, jump hooks, jump shots, or underneath shots.

At least 80 lessons are possible combining the shots with the fakes and other options; 160 if you practice with each hand.

General Directions

1. Start in the half down position with the ball at waist height.

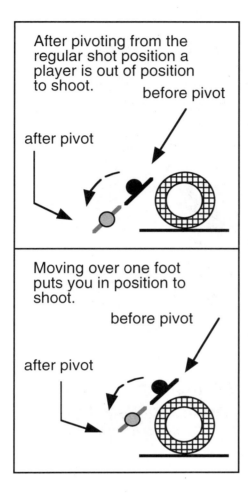

After pivoting from the regular shot position a player is out of position to shoot.

before pivot

after pivot

Moving over one foot puts you in position to shoot.

before pivot

after pivot

2. Five one foot shots are taken from each of the three positions using the backboard, even in the center position. The positions (as they will be referred to) are right, center, and left of the basket.

3. The order of shooting is from right, to center, to left (opposite for lefties).

4. Use the left foot first as pivot foot in each position and then the right foot.

5. Players shoot 30 shots per lesson: five shots at each of the 3 positions pivoting with the left foot and then 5 at each position using the right foot.

6. Players square up to the spot on the backboard where they aim. For hook shots, squaring up means that the shoulders and the ball are in line with the spot on the backboard where you aim.

7. When starting with the back to the basket, players set up slightly to the right (the court right, not your right) when pivoting with the right foot or slightly to the left when using the left foot. This puts players in a normal shooting position after they pivot.

8. I encourage even beginners to practice some of these lessons with the opposite hand. Repeat each lesson completely with the other hand.

9. Backward *in directions always means that you move in the direction that your back is facing. It does not mean toward or away from the basket.* Forward *means that you move in the direction you face.*

10. Left *always means that you move toward the left side of the court.* Right *means move toward the right side of the court. These directions are absolute.*

11. Lefties follow the same directions unless stated otherwise as in step 3 above.

Key Points

Players often have a favorite pivot foot. Each lesson is executed first using the left foot and then repeated using the right foot. Practicing with only one pivot foot noticeably detracts from a player's effectiveness.

Do not practice with just the right hand on the right side and the left hand on the left side. Practice all moves with your normal shooting hand on both sides of the basket. If you want to shoot with your opposite hand, then practice this way on both sides as well. This doubles the amount of practice.

Pivot forward to face the basket. Left foot pivot.

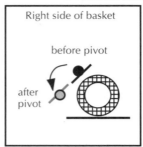

Right side of basket

before pivot

after pivot

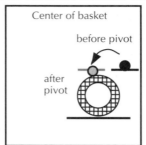

Center of basket

before pivot

after pivot

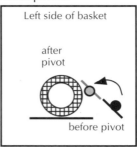

Left side of basket

after pivot

before pivot

Pivot forward to face the basket. Right foot pivot.

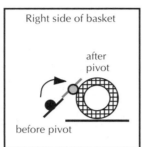

Right side of basket

after pivot

before pivot

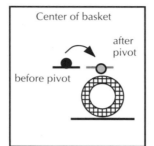

Center of basket

after pivot

before pivot

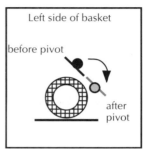

Left side of basket

before pivot

after pivot

2 Pivot Around Shoot

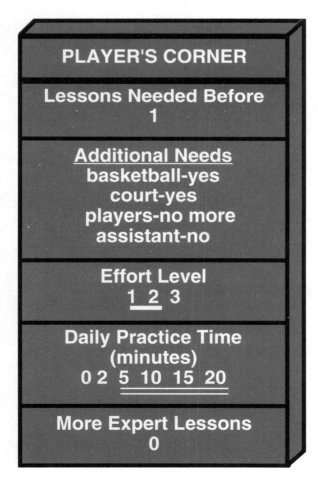

PLAYER'S CORNER

Lessons Needed Before
1

Additional Needs
basketball-yes
court-yes
players-no more
assistant-no

Effort Level
1 2 3

Daily Practice Time
(minutes)
0 2 5 10 15 20

More Expert Lessons
0

Brief:

Starting with the back to the basket, a player pivots forward to face the basket and takes a one foot shot.

Why Do This

In a game this shot is taken after both rebounding or picking up a loose ball under the basket. It is a template for many other moves, some further from the basket, involving various fakes. It is an important offensive move. Practice this move slowly at first.

Directions

1. Start with the back to the basket on the right side pivoting on the left foot. Move one step toward the left so that after pivoting you are in position to shoot.

2. Raise the ball overhead and then pivot forward to face the basket. Square up, then shoot.

3. When pivoting on the right foot, set up one foot to the right to be in position to shoot.

Key Points

1. Do this slowly at first.

2. Raise the ball overhead before you pivot. This is a slight exaggeration of the real motion, which involves turning and bringing the ball up simultaneously. However, bringing the ball up sooner prevents a player from becoming tied up while the ball is still low.

3. Read Lesson 1. There are 30-60 shots in this lesson.

How to Practice

Read lesson 1.

Pivot backward to face the basket. Left foot pivot.

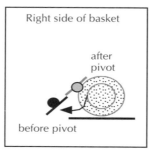
Right side of basket
before pivot
after pivot

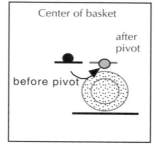
Center of basket
before pivot
after pivot

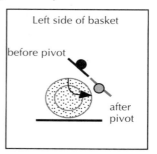
Left side of basket
after pivot
before pivot

Pivot backward to face the basket. Right foot pivot.

Right side of basket
after pivot
before pivot

Center of basket
after pivot
before pivot

Left side of basket
before pivot
after pivot

3 Pivot Backward Shoot

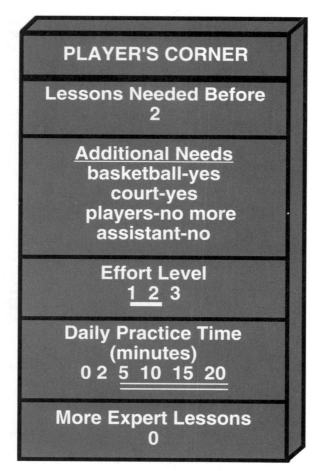

PLAYER'S CORNER

Lessons Needed Before
2

Additional Needs
basketball-yes
court-yes
players-no more
assistant-no

Effort Level
1 2 3

Daily Practice Time
(minutes)
0 2 5 10 15 20

More Expert Lessons
0

Brief:

This is the same as Lesson 2 except you pivot around backward.

Why Do This

A player needs to know how to make a move in either pivot direction. Often the ball is loose underneath, and this is the best way to turn. Lesson 2 covers pivoting forward (like walking forward), while this lesson covers pivoting backward (like walking backward).

Directions

1. Start with the back to the basket. Set up one foot to the left when pivoting with the left foot and one to the right when pivoting with the right foot.

2. Push the ball overhead, then pivot backward toward the basket.

3. Square up and shoot.

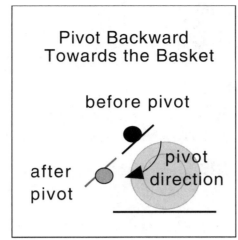

Pivot Backward
Towards the Basket

before pivot

after
pivot

pivot
direction

Key Points

1. Read Lesson 1.

2. See the diagrams. There are 30-60 shots in this lesson.

4 Step Fake Shoot

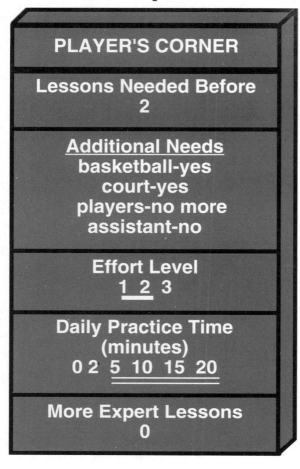

PLAYER'S CORNER

Lessons Needed Before
2

Additional Needs
basketball-yes
court-yes
players-no more
assistant-no

Effort Level
1 2 3

**Daily Practice Time
(minutes)**
0 2 5 10 15 20

More Expert Lessons
0

Brief:
Facing the basket each player fakes, squares up, then shoots.

Why Do This
This lesson introduces faking and shooting together. Use this move at any distance from the basket. The step fake is used in many other lessons in this section as well in many other situations.

Directions
1. Face the basket in the half down position with the ball at waist height. Keep the ball at waist height initially. Move it high or low on the fake when you are more expert.

2. The step fake entails slowly pushing the ball in a direction away from the pivot foot while simultaneously stepping in the same direction. Increase the step part of the fake as you become more expert.

Step Fake Shoot. Left foot pivot.

⟶ Direction of step fake   ● Pivot foot

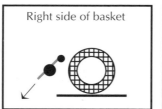
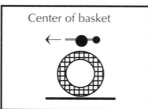
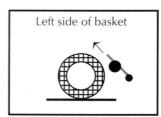

Step Fake Shoot. Right foot pivot.

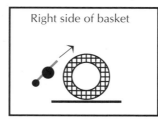
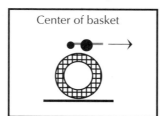
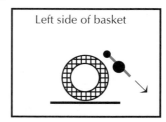

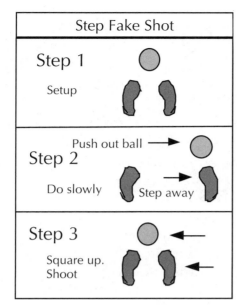

Step Fake Shot
Step 1 Setup
Step 2 Push out ball → Do slowly / Step away
Step 3 Square up. Shoot

3. After the fake bring the feet back to shoulder width; move the ball overhead while stepping back; square up, and shoot.

4. Shoot 5 shots from the right, the center, and then the left. Switch the pivot foot and repeat.

Key Points

1. The fake is slow, even in a game situation. The move after the fake is at normal speed. Both are done slowly in this lesson. Speeding up this move makes learning more difficult. You will naturally speed up as your balance improves.

2. Shift the body weight to the stepping foot on the fake and then back to the pivot foot on the recoil. Distribute weight evenly on the shot.

3. The length of the step varies with the use of this move. Take a short step fake before shooting. If you want to reverse direction to drive or shoot, a longer step may work better. Don't worry about these things now. You will find plenty of uses for this move once you execute it smoothly.

4. Read lesson 1. There are 30-60 shots involved in this lesson.

5 Fake Pivot Shoot

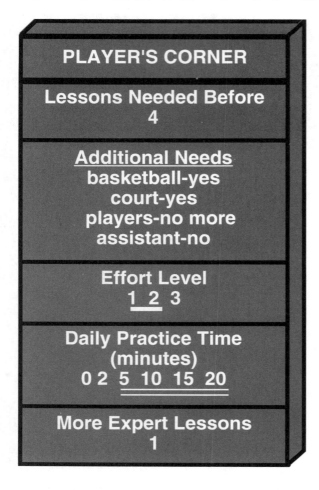

PLAYER'S CORNER

Lessons Needed Before
4

Additional Needs
basketball-yes
court-yes
players-no more
assistant-no

Effort Level
1 _2_ 3

**Daily Practice Time
(minutes)**
0 2 5 10 15 20

More Expert Lessons
1

Brief:
The step fake is made with the back to the basket. Then pivot around forward and shoot.

Why Do This
This is a smart and effective use for the step fake. The defense will move both feet in the direction of the fake and then you quickly spin (pivot) around away from them, square up and shoot. Usually the defensive player will not recover quickly enough. This will leave you open to shoot, pass, or dribble. In this lesson you shoot. Use this move at any distance from the basket, but practice at a distance of one foot.

Directions
1. Set up in the half down position with the back to the basket, the ball at waist height. Start 1-2 steps to the left, so that when you pivot around right, you will be in a good position to shoot.

2. Simultaneously push the ball away and step away from the pivot foot; this is a step fake.

3. Pivot 180 degrees forward to face the basket. Raise the ball overhead as you pivot; square up and shoot.

4. Shoot 5 shots from the right, the center, and then the left. Switch the pivot foot and repeat.

Key Points
1. The fake is slow, even in a game situation. The move after the fake is at normal speed. Both are done slowly in this lesson. Speeding up this move makes learning more difficult. You will naturally speed up as your balance improves.

2. Shift the body weight to the stepping foot on the fake and then back to the pivot foot on the pivot.

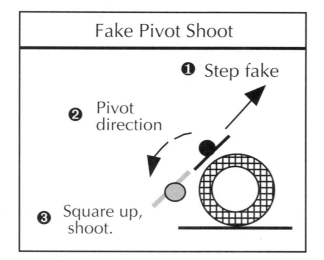

Fake Pivot Shoot
❶ Step fake
❷ Pivot direction
❸ Square up, shoot.

3. The length of the step again varies with the use of this move.

4. Read lesson 1. There are 30-60 shots involved in this lesson.

More Expert Lessons

Fake Pivot Backward

1. Repeat this lesson pivoting backward instead of forward.

2. With the back to the basket step fake away from the pivot foot, pivot around backward to face the basket, square up and shoot.

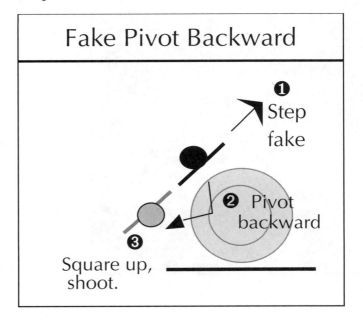

6 Pivot Fake Shoot

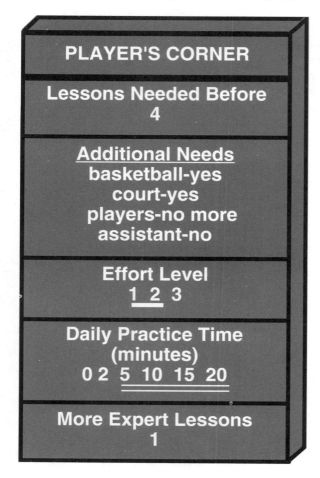

PLAYER'S CORNER

Lessons Needed Before
4

Additional Needs
basketball-yes
court-yes
players-no more
assistant-no

Effort Level
1 2 3

Daily Practice Time
(minutes)
0 2 5 10 15 20

More Expert Lessons
1

Brief:

Facing the basket a player pivots forward 180 degrees and then step fakes before pivoting back to the original position facing the basket.

Why Do This

This lesson combines faking, pivoting, and shooting. This is a common sequence with college and professional players. It can be used in many situations both close to or far from the basket to evade the defense before shooting, passing, or dribbling.

Directions

1. Face the basket with the ball at waist height in the half down position.

2. Pivot forward 180 degrees so that your back is to the basket. Push the ball to the outside as you pivot. This looks like a step fake after you pivot.

3. Pivot backward to the original position facing the basket, holding the ball high.

4. Square up and shoot.

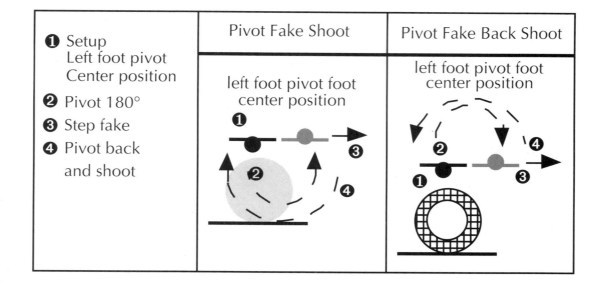

❶ Setup Left foot pivot Center position ❷ Pivot 180° ❸ Step fake ❹ Pivot back and shoot	Pivot Fake Shoot	Pivot Fake Back Shoot

Key Points

1. Start with a short pivot and step fake; this is the pivot fake. Increase the step part of the fake as you become more accustomed to this move.

2. When you pivot back to face the basket, keep the ball close to the body as you bring it overhead.

3. Do this from the right, left, and center positions with the left and then the right foot as pivot foot—30 shots.

More Expert Lessons

Pivot Fake Back Shoot

Perform this lesson initially pivoting 180 degrees backward instead of forward. Then pivot forward, not backward, to the original position facing the basket. Keep the ball close to the body as you bring it high.

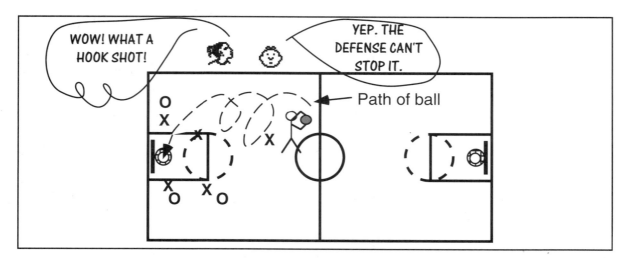

7 Hook Shot 1-2

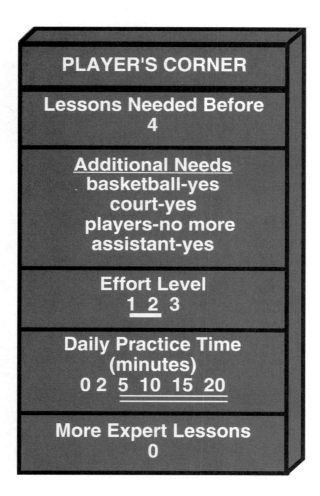

PLAYER'S CORNER

Lessons Needed Before
4

Additional Needs
basketball-yes
court-yes
players-no more
assistant-yes

Effort Level
1 2 3

**Daily Practice Time
(minutes)**
0 2 5 10 15 20

More Expert Lessons
0

Brief:

In Part 1 you learn how to square up for the hook shot. In Part 2 start with your back to the basket and then face the basket.

Why Do This

•Hook shots, unlike other shots are usually used close to the basket under great defensive pressure. The power of the hook is that it neutralizes the defense. It allows players unimpeded 1-2 foot shots with the defense right in their faces.

•Two reasons stand out for the effectiveness of the hook. One, the body of the shooter protects the ball from the defense. Second the hook is a quick shot. Players need not even turn around to face the basket to shoot.

•The more awkward the position, the more effective the shot. Besides shooting the hook from the right, center and left positions, execute it starting from a position facing the basket and with the back to the basket. The only difference in these shots is the direction of the pivot. Facing forward the pivot is a half turn backward; with the back to the basket the pivot is a half turn forward.

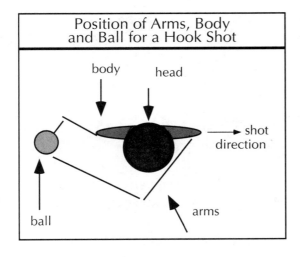

Position of Arms, Body and Ball for a Hook Shot

body   head

shot direction

ball   arms

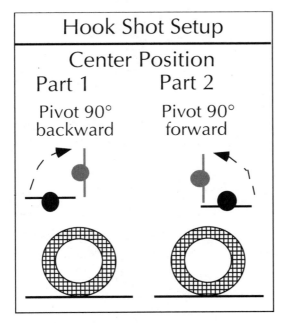

Hook Shot Setup

Center Position

Part 1   **Part 2**

Pivot 90°   Pivot 90°
backward   forward

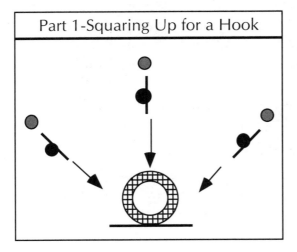

Part 1-Squaring Up for a Hook

•Hook shots are not for novices. One, to be effective you must control the ball with one hand. This is difficult for young players with small hands. Two, hook shots are primarily used close to the basket when the defense is tight. With novices the defense is often not tight. My advice is to wait until you need this shot. It will take one to several months to perfect it.

•Even though the hook is always shot off the same foot (right handers use the left foot, left handers, the right foot), players initially standing on the opposite pivot foot take a step hook (Lesson 9). A right hander on the right foot (actually, the wrong foot in this situation) takes a step with the left foot. The shot is taken as usual off the left foot.

•All lessons are given for right handers. Left handers follow the same directions using the other pivot foot and arm.

•As with the other shooting lessons, players line up one foot from the basket on the right, then center, and then left. Since the hook is a short, quick, effective shot, I recommend that you practice with each hand. This means twice as much practice.

•Always use the backboard and square up to the backboard.

•Two types of hooks are especially effective. One is the jump hook (See Lesson 8). This has the advantage of the ball being released higher and closer to the basket. It is a quick flick of the wrist. This shot is more difficult to block. The other type of hook is taken from directly underneath the basket (See Lesson 10). This hook enables players to shoot without needing to take steps outward, turn around, and square up. It also catches the defense by surprise because it is an awkward position to shoot from. The net and the rim are also often in the way of the defense.

Directions

Part 1

1. Start with the ball at waist height; left foot pivot foot. From one foot away on the right side, face the basket.

2. Turn sideways so that the shooting arm and the ball are straight out to the side, not in front of the body. Both shoulders and the ball are in a straight line. The left elbow is forward and slightly up. The right elbow is back and slightly down.

3. Squaring up on a hook shot is accomplished by aligning the ball and the shoulders in a straight line with the point on the backboard that you are aiming at.

4. Hook the ball directly overhead. A common error is to loop the ball in front of the body. In this position the ball is not protected by the body. It is easy for the defense to block the shot.

5. Repeat each move 5 times; 15 shots total. Move to the center and then the left. Use the backboard from each position.

Part 2

6. Start with your back to the basket 1-2 feet to the left of your position in Part 1. Pivot 90 degrees (a quarter turn) forward, square up, and shoot. Repeat 5 times from each position; 15 shots total.

7. Start from a position facing the basket. Rotate a quarter turn backward, square up, and shoot. Repeat from each position; 15 shoots total.

Key Points

1. Shoot the hook shot with the ball directly on the side, not forward.

2. The shoulders and the ball are in line with the shooting direction.

3. Square up to the spot on the backboard that you are aiming at.

4. The body protects the ball from the defense.

5. Shooting the ball from a position in front of your body shoves it right in front of the defensive player.

6. The hook is mostly a wrist shot. It is a quick flick. Repeating Lesson 2 for 1-2 minutes before you practice helps.

7. It will probably take a month of practice to execute an effective hook. Be patient.

How to Practice

Wait until you are ready. Then practice everyday until you are an expert. When you are more expert, go to Lessons 8-10, which also involve the hook.

8 Jump Hook & Fake

Brief:

Two moves shown here , a jump and a fake, make a hook more effective.

Why Do This

This lesson is identical to Lesson 19 except that you jump when shooting the hook. In a jump hook the ball is released from a higher position than in the regular hook. More wrist and less arm are used as well. Because quickness of release makes this shot effective, in a game you will probably square up in the air or not square up at all when using it. Often players use it immediately after a rebound, just before the defense moves to you.

Directions

1. Start on the right side of the basket squared up to take a hook shot.

2. Raise the ball 1-2 feet straight up and slightly toward the basket.

3. Jump and flick the wrist to shoot the jump hook. You do not need to use the backboard.

Key Points

1. When you are more experienced, extend yourself completely on this hook.

2. Shoot 5 shots from the right, center, and left.

3. Flick the ball quickly using your wrist, not your arms.

4. It is okay to flick the ball on the way up rather than wait to reach the peak of your jump.

More Expert Lessons

Facing & with Back to Basket

1. Repeat this lesson starting from a position facing the basket.

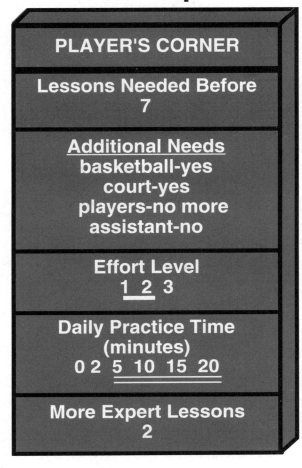

Release of the Ball

| regular hook | jump hook |

shot direction

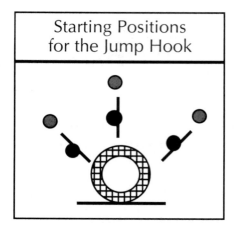

Starting Positions for the Jump Hook

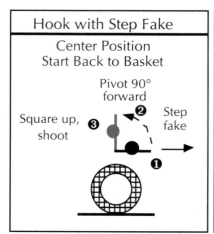

Hook with Step Fake

Center Position
Start Back to Basket

Pivot 90° forward

Square up, shoot

Step fake

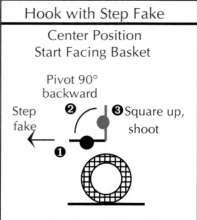

Hook with Step Fake

Center Position
Start Facing Basket

Pivot 90° backward

Step fake

Square up, shoot

2. Jump, rotate a quarter turn backward, and square up while in the air before shooting.

3. Take 5 shots from the right, center, and left.

4. Repeat the above, starting with your back to the basket; jump, rotate, and square up while in the air; this sequence requires another 15 shots.

Hook or Jump Hook with Step Fake

1. Both the hook and the jump hook can be practiced with the step fake explained in Lesson 16.

2. The fake involves pushing the ball and stepping away from the pivot foot.

3. Then pivot a quarter turn, square up, and shoot.

4. The left foot is always the pivot foot (right for lefties).

5. Do each shot from the right, center, and left positions.

6. Another lesson involves practicing from positions first facing and then with the back to the basket.

How To Practice

Go slowly. Stay with the more basic moves until you are very comfortable. Don't overpractice. It will take a while to feel comfortable doing these.

9 Step Hook & Fake

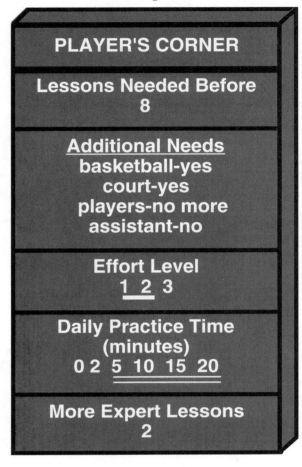

PLAYER'S CORNER

Lessons Needed Before
8

Additional Needs
basketball-yes
court-yes
players-no more
assistant-no

Effort Level
1 **2** 3

Daily Practice Time
(minutes)
0 2 5 10 15 20

More Expert Lessons
2

Brief:

You shoot a hook starting on the opposite pivot foot: right foot for righties, left foot for lefties.

Why Do This

It is difficult to take a hook off the right foot if you are right handed. So, when the right foot is the pivot foot, you need to take a step to the left foot before shooting. This is why a hook shot with the right foot as pivot is called a step hook for right handers. For lefties the words left and right above need to be switched.

Directions

1. With your back toward the basket, stand in the half down position 2 feet from the basket with the ball waist high.

2. Pivot on the right foot a quarter turn backward.

3. Step on the left foot, square up, and shoot.

4. Shoot 5 shots from the left, center, and right. Shoot 15 shots total.

5. Now face the basket, pivot on the right foot a quarter turn forward, step on the left foot, square up, and shoot. Again, shoot 5 shots from each position–right, center, and left–15 total.

Key Points

1. Start with the right foot as pivot foot (left for lefties).

2. A step hook means that you step onto the left foot and then take a regular hook shot.

More Expert Lessons

Fake Step Hook

A fake makes the step hook a more effective move. Fake by moving the ball and the body in one direction and then stepping away in the other direction. The fake is different depending

Step Hook

❶ Right pivot foot center position

❷ Pivot 90° and step

❸ Square up and shoot

Back to basket

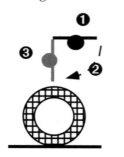

Facing the basket

on whether you start facing or with your back to the basket. The right foot is always the pivot foot (left foot for lefties); take the step fake away from the pivot foot.

1. If you start facing the basket, step fake to your left then pivot forward a quarter turn. Square up, and shoot.

2. If you start with your back to the basket, step fake again to your left (this is to the right of the court). Pivot backward one quarter turn toward the basket. Square up and shoot.

3. Repeat each move from the right, center, and left positions; 30 shots total.

Jump Step Hook with Fake

Repeat the step hook with fake using the jump hook. Start with the back to the basket and then face the basket.

Step Hook with Fake

❶ Right pivot foot Center position

❷ Step fake

❸ Pivot 90° and step

❹ Square up and shoot

Back to basket

Facing the basket

10 Underneath Hooks

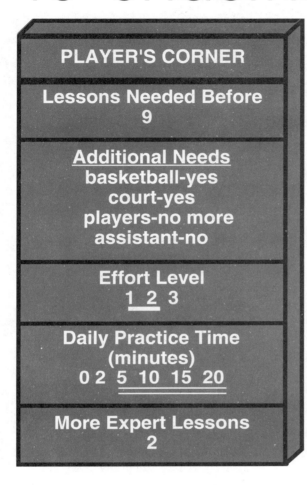

PLAYER'S CORNER

Lessons Needed Before
9

Additional Needs
basketball-yes
court-yes
players-no more
assistant-no

Effort Level
1 2 3

**Daily Practice Time
(minutes)**
0 2 5 10 15 20

More Expert Lessons
2

Brief:
You shoot from directly underneath the basket.

Why Do This

It is useful to possess the ability to shoot a hook from directly under the basket. Picking up a loose ball or a rebound in traffic may not give you much time or room to move. These hooks can be shot in awkward and crowded situations. Practice each move at least 5 times in a row from as many directions as possible.

Directions

1. Stand directly behind the basket under the backboard facing the court.

2. Using the left foot as the pivot foot, take a half step forward with the right foot toward the right side of the basket. A half step means you step in a direction but do not bring your foot down until you shoot.

3. Shoot a hook shot off the backboard. This looks like a backward hook.

4. Take 5 shoots moving in each direction from the basket–right, center, left.

Key Points

1. It may take some time before you get the knack.

2. Use the backboard on the left and right sides. It is okay to go right over the rim from the center.

3. If you are having difficulty, start with both feet on the ground in the best position to shoot the underneath hook. When you are more expert take the step.

4. Take 5 shots in each direction.

More Expert Lessons

Step Underneath Hook

Repeat the previous move, starting with the right foot as pivot foot. Then take a step hook in any direction. This shot may be easier since the step places you in a better position.

Underneath the Basket Hooks

Stand directly under the basket, not the backboard, facing the right sideline. Move toward either sideline or the center of the court. Take a hook, jump hook, or step hook. Facing the left sideline or the center, you can make the same moves.

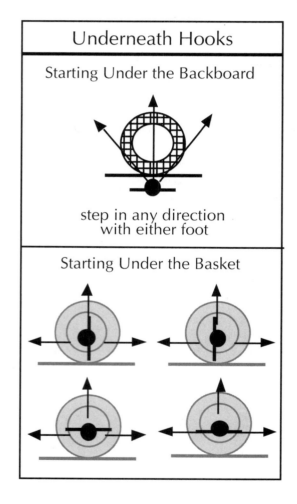

11 Jump Shot

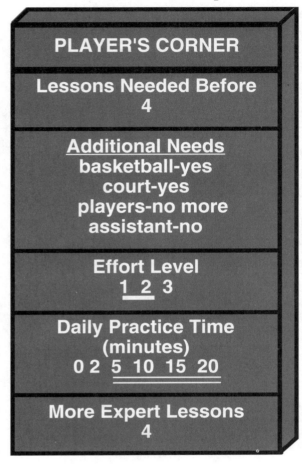

PLAYER'S CORNER

Lessons Needed Before
4

Additional Needs
basketball-yes
court-yes
players-no more
assistant-no

Effort Level
1 _2_ 3

**Daily Practice Time
(minutes)**
0 2 _5 10 15 20_

More Expert Lessons
4

Brief:

You shoot a one foot jump shot from the right, center, and left of the basket.

Why Do This

A big advantage of the jump shot over a stationary shot is that you can square up and adjust to the defense while you are in the air. You can more easily shoot on the move and also shoot, or get the shot off, more quickly. Another advantage is that the ball is released from a higher position. Historically the jump shot has revolutionized the game.

When you first learn the jump shot, you just jump and shoot. It's okay to shoot on the way up. Jump shots in games are released at every elevation and any instant—on the way up, at the top, and on the way down.

•On the way up is the most comfortable way to shoot a shot from a distance or to quickly shoot before the defense can react.

•Shoot at the top of the jump when the defense is close or you are near the basket.

•The on the way down position is used when someone is "in your face." Along with the fade away, this is a more difficult shot.

Directions

1. Start with the left foot as pivot foot, ball at waist height. Set up one foot from the basket on the right side.

2. Bring the ball overhead; square up; jump and shoot on the way up.

3. Shoot 5 shots from the right, center, and then left. Switch your pivot foot and repeat. Thirty shots total.

Key Points

1. Just jump and shoot. When you are more expert, you can easily work on fadeaways, quick releases, maximum height releases, as well as combinations of other moves and fakes.

2. You shoot jump shots with the defense close, so practice the basics with close defense before spending time on all-world moves. See Lesson 15, Defense in Face Shoot.

3. Practice all of these moves from one foot, not 2 or 3 or 10 feet. Shooting is 50-90% shooting technique. The farther you go from the basket, the better the chance you lose technique.

More Expert Lessons

Step Fake Jump Shot

Repeat this lesson, taking a step fake away from the pivot foot before you shoot.

Ball Fake Jump Shot

Repeat this lesson, making a ball fake toward the pivot foot. This is a more difficult fake to learn.

Fake Turn Around

This is the same as Lesson 18 except that you jump. Practice it pivoting both forward and backward. This is a very effective move with tight defense.

Pump Fake

1. Pump or push the ball upward just before you are about to shoot. Flick the wrists like you are going to shoot. Remember that fakes are slow compared to the actual shot, so that the defense can react.

2. You also act like you are going to jump by slightly bending the knees and straightening them out when you pump.

3. Practice this fake two ways:

- Start with the ball at waist height.
- Start with the ball overhead.

4. Often you can pump it several times to get the defense in the air.

5. After the defense jumps, take your regular shot.

6. This move is primarily for older players. Practice it from the right, center, and left of the basket.

- I must add a note of caution—a quick release is usually much more effective than a pump fake. In isolated circumstances against a very reactive quick athletic defense, the pump may get players off their feet. You shoot or jump when he is on the way down, and you can expect to be fouled often.

12 Pressure Shot

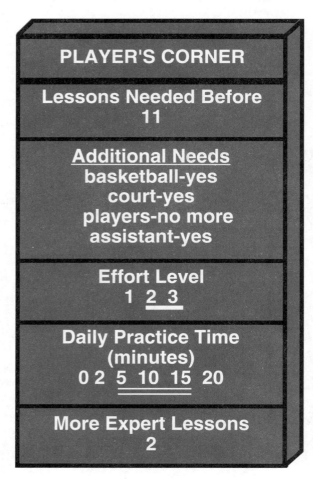

PLAYER'S CORNER

Lessons Needed Before
11

Additional Needs
basketball-yes
court-yes
players-no more
assistant-yes

Effort Level
1 <u>2</u> 3

**Daily Practice Time
(minutes)**
0 2 <u>5</u> <u>10</u> <u>15</u> 20

More Expert Lessons
2

Brief:
You place a ball on the floor under the basket, then quickly pick it up and shoot.

Why Do This

This lesson simulates shooting under game-like pressure. While grabbing the ball off the floor, you position the feet, as well as the body, to shoot. Execute the first part of the move quickly; set up and shoot slowly. Most novices tend to shoot too quickly and end up missing easy shots. Game situations are a piece of cake after this; you will concentrate more readily and play better. A caution—this lesson may destroy a novice's shooting technique if he/she shoots too quickly.

Directions

1. Stand directly under the basket.

2. Place the ball on the floor one foot away from the basket so that it does not roll. Stand up and take one step back in any direction. If you step back under the basket, the lesson is a little more difficult.

3. Quickly go for the ball and grab it. Set up and take the shot slowly. You do not need to jump much even if you are taking a jump shot.

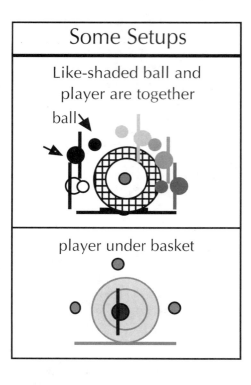
4. To increase the pressure and make this lesson more game-like, instruct an assistant or another player to urge (yell at) you to move more quickly.

5. Repeat this 5 to 10 times, regularly changing the direction that you face.

6. Now, put the ball directly under the basket, step away and repeat 5-10 times.

Key Points

1. This lesson is not for novices because shooting too quickly may destroy developing shooting technique.

2. No dribbling.

3. Go for the ball quickly. Then set up and shoot more slowly. Do not miss any shots. If you do, repeat Lesson 23 completely for each shot missed.

4. Make sure to square up and not to walk.

5. More advanced players can try underneath hooks instead of regular shots.

6. It is helpful if an assistant urges or harasses you to shoot too fast. This adds pressure. Of course you should not react to it. Shoot the ball slowly or at normal speed. Do nothing quickly except get possession of the ball.

More Expert Lessons

Pressure Shot with D

A manager (or another player) stands nearby and harasses you. Harassing means that they bother the shooter but do not interfere with the shot. Here are some harassing maneuvers:

1. Shout at the player.

2. Wave arms around.

3. Move body close to the shooter.

4. Wave arms to obstruct the vision of the shooter. The hands come no closer than 6 inches to the face. Moving hands closer is dangerous as well as against the rules.

Pressure Shot Two

1. Players set up, side to side, with legs and elbows touching within 2 yards or even underneath the basket.

2. Place the ball on the floor 2-3 feet away. Go for the ball at a signal; an assistant can yell, "Go."

3. Get position by stepping in front of the other player first, and then go for the ball second.

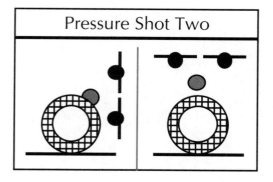

Pressure Shot Two

4. The player that acquires the ball shoots; the other player is on defense.

5. The job of the defense is to harass the shooter without fouling. Complete several defensive lessons like Lessons 67 and 751 from The Player's Bible first.

13 Run Stop Shoot

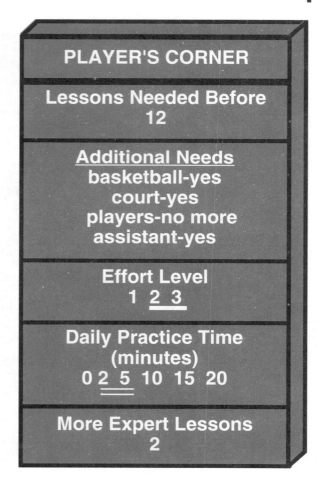

PLAYER'S CORNER

Lessons Needed Before
12

Additional Needs
basketball-yes
court-yes
players-no more
assistant-yes

Effort Level
1 2 3

Daily Practice Time
(minutes)
0 2 5 10 15 20

More Expert Lessons
2

Brief:

Sprint to the basket for the ball, pick it up quickly, and then shoot slowly.

Why Do This

When players must sprint before shooting, they often shoot the ball just as quickly as they sprint. The result is that they miss many easy shots. This lesson slows you down to shoot after a sprint to the basket.

Directions

1. Place the ball under the basket and set up at the top of the key.

2. Sprint for the ball, pick it up and stop, then take the shot in a relaxed, unhurried way.

3. Get the rebound, place the ball on the floor near the basket, then return to the top of the key.

4. Repeat 5-10 times.

Key Points

1. Sprint all out for the ball.

2. Slow down after gaining possession of it.

3. Shoot at a normal, unhurried speed.

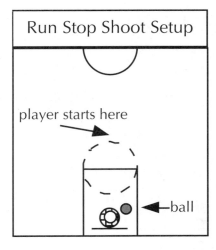

Run Stop Shoot Setup

player starts here

ball

4. It is helpful to have an assistant urge you to do things more quickly than you should.

More Expert Lessons

Run Stop Shoot with D

Another player or assistant harasses the shooter. Harassing means that they bother the shooter but do not interfere with the shot. Here are some harassing maneuvers:

1. Shout at the player.

2. Wave arms around.

3. Move body close to the shooter.

4. Wave arms to obstruct the vision of the shooter. The hands come no closer than 6 inches to the face. Moving hands closer is dangerous as well as against the rules.

Run Catch Shoot

1. You start a cut to the basket from near midcourt. Another player in one corner of the court passes the ball so that it meets you at the basket.

2. Catch the ball at the basket, slow down, and then shoot.

3. Repeat 5-10 times.

4. Another person stationed under the boards can harass you on the shot.

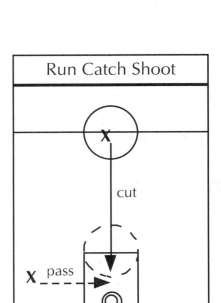

Run Catch Shoot

X

cut

X pass

14 Catch Up

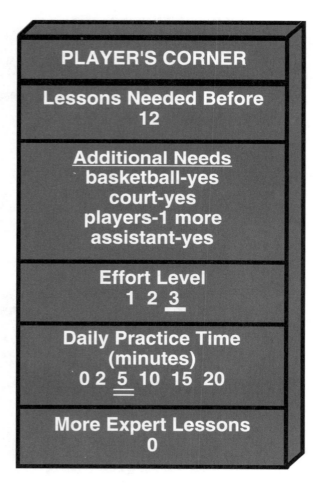

PLAYER'S CORNER

Lessons Needed Before
12

Additional Needs
basketball-yes
court-yes
players-1 more
assistant-yes

Effort Level
1 2 <u>3</u>

Daily Practice Time
(minutes)
0 2 <u>5</u> 10 15 20

More Expert Lessons
0

Brief:

A defensive player sprints to catch the offensive player driving to the basket.

Why Do This

The defense learns to hustle while the offense shoots under game-like pressure. Game situations are easier for the offense after this lesson. The defense learns not to commit flagrant and unnecessary fouls when they are not in position to stop the offense.

Directions

1. The offensive player sets up at midcourt with the ball. The defense sets up one step behind.

2. The offensive player has five seconds to take off to the basket, dribbling the ball.

3. After the offense takes one step, the defense takes off in pursuit.

4. The offense sprints to the basket and then shoots the layup slowly. If the defense catches up, the offense stops and takes a short shot.

5. The defense needs to go 3 feet past the offense and then step in front to prevent the

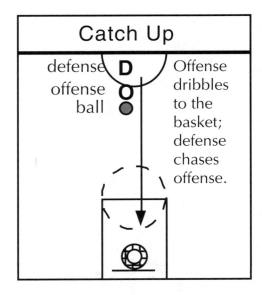

Catch Up

defense **D**
offense **O**
ball ●

Offense dribbles to the basket; defense chases offense.

layup. If the defense is not able to go past the offense, then they can only harass from a distance.

6. Go for the rebound, whether or not the shot is missed. Box out, if you know how.

Key Points

1. The offensive player must slow down on the last step.

2. If the defense beats the offense, then the offense should stop and take a short shot rather than a layup.

3. The defense must not run right in front of the offense. To avoid blocking fouls and collisions, the defense must run at least 3 feet ahead of the offense, step in front, and then stop.

4. The defense should not reach for the ball from the side instead of exerting the effort needed to run past the offense. The defense must try to catch up and, at least, get the rebound.

15 Defense in Face Shoot

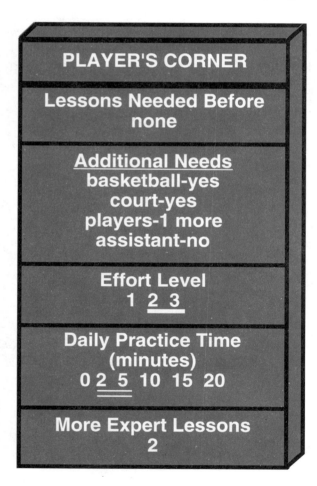

PLAYER'S CORNER

Lessons Needed Before
none

Additional Needs
basketball-yes
court-yes
players-1 more
assistant-no

Effort Level
1 <u>2</u> 3

Daily Practice Time
(minutes)
0 <u>2 5</u> 10 15 20

More Expert Lessons
2

Brief:
The offense shoots a one foot shot with the defense in their face.

Why Do This

The offense shoots with defensive harassment from up close. Initially the defense neither touches the ball nor the offense. It takes effort to maneuver out of the way of the shot, especially when the defense is a foot taller.

Directions

1. The offense takes a normal one foot shot or jump shot using the backboard.

2. The defense stands 3-4 inches away directly between shooter and the basket with hands outstretched harassing the shooter. One hand is in the face (eyes), no closer than six inches, impairing vision of the basket. This hand can move. The other hand is outstretched straight up to block the ball. This hand is stationary; do not slash forward at the ball. Yelling and talking about relatives enhances the harassment.

3. The defense does not block the shot. Move your hands so that the shot is not deflected.

4. Offense and defense can switch roles after each shot.

Defense in the Face

The defense must place one hand in the offense's line of view.

line of view

Key Points

1. The defense may jump with the offense.

2. The defense acts like it is going to block the shot but does not block it.

3. One arm on defense is extended straight up. The other arm is in the face.

4. No flailing of the arms.

5. The defense wants to impair the vision of the offense. The hand in the face is between the shooter's eyes and the basket.

More Expert Lessons

Defense in Face Rebound

Both players go for the rebound whether or not the shot is made. Each player boxes the other out. Switch roles after each shot.

Shooting When Fouled

Often fouls under the basket are not called. You need to make these shots even though you are fouled. If the foul is called so much the better. Let an assistant do the fouling. The fouls are soft pushes on the shooting arm and shoulders. As you adjust, the fouls should increase in intensity.

16 Pivoting with Ball

Brief:

Pivot while moving the ball high and low, left and right, and close and far from the body.

Why Do This

Pivoting, as previously discussed, is applicable to everything done with the basketball. This lesson combines pivoting with ball movement. You can use the ball movement to keep the ball away from opponents as well as fake before either shooting, passing, or dribbling. This skill is the key to all offensive moves.

Directions

1. Hold the ball at waist height, feet shoulder width apart. The left foot is the pivot foot.

2. Take one long step to the right and push the ball to the far right, low to the ground. The ball is to the right of your foot.

3. Pivot 180 degrees forward, halfway around, and simultaneously push the ball high overhead.

4. Repeat this twice forward and then twice pivoting backward.

5. Switch the pivot foot and repeat pivoting forward and backward.

6. Repeat the entire lesson several times. Take longer steps as you become more expert.

Key Points

1. Pushing the ball is a quick powerful movement.

2. Use these verbal cues as you do the lesson: stretch low, pivot high.

3. Initially concentrate on learning the routine. Gradually work to improve the movements.

How to Practice

Most lessons in this book involve pivoting. The applications are almost endless. Novices cannot practice this enough at the beginning of the season. Do it for homework or during any warm-up. All offensive moves start here. That is why this is such a pivotal lesson.

we've got videos and clinics

THE BASKETBALL COACH'S BIBLE WILL HELP YOU BY ...

✴ showing you how best to plan and run practice
✴ supplying two hundred field tested lessons ready to use
✴ systematically teaching each skill, step-by-step
✴ not skipping basic steps essential to your success
✴ presenting strategies, a warm down, game statistics and more
✴ saving you time by giving you methods and ideas that work

books

A. **The Basketball Coach's Bible**   350 pages
  Everything about coaching. (07-5) $24.95

B. **The Basketball Player's Bible**   270 pages
  All individual fundamentals. (13-X) $19.95

C. **The Basketball Shooting Guide** 45 pages
  Yields permanent improvement. (14-8) $ 6.95

D. **The Basketball Scoring Guide**   47 pages
  Teaches pro moves step-by-step. (15-6) $ 6.95

E. **The Basketball Dribbling Guide** 46 pages
  Anyone can be a good dribbler. (16-4) $ 6.95

F. **The Basketball Defense Guide**   46 pages
  Defense in every situation. (17-2) $ 6.95

G. **The Basketball Pass Cut Catch Guide** 47 pages
  Be an effective team player. (18-0) $ 6.95

H. **Basketball Fundamentals**   46 pages
  Covers all fundamentals. (08-3) $ 6.95

I. **Planning Basketball Practice**   46 pages
  Use time effectively, plan, plus. (09-1) $ 6.95

J. 9 **Book Series**, A - I (01-6)   ~$20 off $ 81.50 w/ship

K. 2 **Book Bible Set**, A,B (20-2)   ~$5 off $ 46.13 w/ship

L. 7 **Guide Set**, C - I (21-0)   ~ $5 off $ 49.50 w/ship

videos
40-60 MINUTES; $24.95 EACH
CHECK FOR AVAILABILITY

1. **Fundamentals I** Over 25 individual skill topics. (77-6)
2. **Fundamentals II** Team Skills, plays & pressure defense (90-3)
3. **Planning Practice I** Daily, weekly, and seasonal planning. (75-X)
4. **Planning Practice II** Get 5 times more out of practice. (76-8)
5. **Shooting I** Technique, Hook, Jump Shot & Layup (78-4)
6. **Shooting II** Foul Shooting, 3-Point Shooting, Driving (79-2)
7. **Shooting III** Shooting under pressure, Scoring Moves, Faking (80-6)
8. **Dribbling** Technique, Position, Protect Ball, Looking Up (81-4)
9. **Defense I** Position, Forcing, Trapping, On Shooter (84-9)
10. **Defense II** lane/Post, overplay, Front, Help, Strong-Weak (85-7)
11. **Passing I** Technique, Overhead, Bounce, Communication (82-2)
12. **Passing II** Cutting, Faking, Passing with Defense (83-0)
13. **Rebounding/Picking** Going for the Ball, Positioning, Boxing out (91-1)
14. **The Transition Game** from Foul Line, Center Jump & Plays (86-5)
15. **Team Offense** Offensive setup, Plays, Pliable Offense (87-3)
16. **Team Defense** Helping Out, Zone Shift, Half Court Trap (88-1)
17. **Full Court Pressure** Offense, Trapping Zone, Out-of-Bounds (89-X)

SIDNEY GOLDSTEIN, MR. BASKETBALL BASICS, TELLS YOU ABOUT HIS BOOKS

"This series is about fundamentals. It is a step back to the basics and a step forward to improved training methods. It is a place to start and to return again and again. No matter what your coaching level, age or sex the fundamentals do not change. You will reap great rewards by recognizing, practicing, and applying them to your situation. Visit our web site for 60 pages of information about our books, more comments from coaches, reviews, discounts, freebies, basketball articles, tips, videos, clinics, and more: I guarantee satisfaction."

clinics

VISIT OUR WEB SITE FOR DATE, TIME, AND LOCATION OF COACH AND PLAYER CLINICS:
www.mrbasketball.net

order form

QTY	ITEM	TITLE	PRICE

SHIPPING
$25 = $5; $50 = $5.75; $75 = $6.50
ADD $1 FOR HOME DELIVERY

DISCOUNTS 50-75% CALL OR CHECK www.mrbasketball.net

SUBTOTAL _____
ADD 7% SALES TAX IN PA _____
SHIPPING _____
TOTAL ORDER _____

ALL BOOKS ARE 8.5x11. ALL GUIDES COST 6.95; NEW EDITIONS COST $7.45 WHEN AVAILABLE. ALL VIDEOS COST $24.95 EACH AND RUN 45-60 MINUTES. ISBN 1-884357-(XX-X) SUFFIX IN PARENTHESIS

HOW TO ORDER
Call **1-800-979-8642**
Use our web site: **www.mrbasketball.net**
Fax PO's to: **215-438-4459**

Use your credit card, send a money order or PO to: **Golden Aura Publishing P.O. Box 41012 Phila., PA 19127-1012**

name _____
address _____
city_____ state_____ zip _____
phone _____
card #_____ exp_____ home zip _____